12 REASONS TO LOVE
BASEBALL

by Tyler Mason

12 STORY LIBRARY

www.12StoryLibrary.com

12-Story Library is an imprint of Bookstaves and Press Room Editions

Produced for 12-Story Library by Red Line Editorial

Photographs ©: Matt Slocum/AP Images, cover, 1; Chas. Gross & Co./Library of Congress, 4; ChameleonsEye/Shutterstock Images, 5; Kamira/Shutterstock Images, 6; Christopher Penler/ Shutterstock Images, 7; Rena Schild/Shutterstock Images, 8, 29; Elise Amendola/AP Images, 9, 28; Larry Goren/Four Seam Images/AP Images, 10; George Grantham Bain Collection/Library of Congress, 11, 27; Ross D. Franklin/AP Images, 12; Jeff Chiu/AP Images, 13; JCS/Icon Sportswire/AP Images, 14; Irwin, La Broad, & Pudlin/Library of Congress, 15; Mike Groll/AP Images, 17, 18; Alan C. Heison/ Shutterstock Images, 19; Kathy Willens/AP Images, 20, 26; Photo Works/Shutterstock Images, 21; Frank Franklin II/AP Images, 22; Gene J. Puskar/AP Images, 23; Lenny Ignelzi/AP Images, 24; Julio Cortez/AP Images, 25

Library of Congress Cataloging-in-Publication Data
Names: Mason, Tyler, author.
Title: 12 reasons to love baseball / by Tyler Mason.
Other titles: Twelve reasons to love baseball
Description: Mankato, MN : 12 Story Library, 2018. | Series: Sports report |
    Includes bibliographical references and index. | Audience: Grade 4 to 6.
Identifiers: LCCN 2016047104 (print) | LCCN 2016052597 (ebook) | ISBN
    9781632354259 (hardcover : alk. paper) | ISBN 9781632354945 (pbk. : alk.
    paper) | ISBN 9781621435464 (hosted e-book)
Subjects: LCSH: Baseball--Juvenile literature.
Classification: LCC GV867.5 .M3856 2018 (print) | LCC GV867.5 (ebook) | DDC
    796.357--dc23
LC record available at https://lccn.loc.gov/2016047104

Printed in China
022017

12 STORY LIBRARY

Access free, up-to-date content on this topic plus a full digital version of this book. Scan the QR code on page 31 or use your school's login at 12StoryLibrary.com.

Table of Contents

Baseball Has a Rich History

Baseball has a long history. The first mention of the game was in 1792. Baseball is similar to two older sports. One is cricket. The other is a game called rounders. Both games involve hitting a ball with a bat and running bases.

Many of baseball's rules haven't changed since 1845. That's when Alexander Joy Cartwright created most of the modern rules. He was an executive with the New York Knickerbocker Base Ball Club. The new rules changed some of the more violent features of the game. They also made it faster and more exciting.

The first baseball league was created in 1857. It was called the National Association of Base Ball Players. Today, the American League and National

The modern form of baseball dates back to the mid-1800s.

BASEBALL AND BLACK HISTORY

In the early 1900s, black people faced segregation in the United States. In baseball, black athletes were not allowed to play with white athletes. On April 15, 1947, Jackie Robinson became the first black player to play in the majors. His debut was one of the most important moments in baseball's long history.

League make up Major League Baseball (MLB). The National League began in 1876. The American League started in 1901.

Baseball's popularity rose in the early 1900s.

More cities across the country had clubs. And stars such as slugger Babe Ruth drew huge crowds.

Baseball is based on the older game of cricket.

Ballparks Are Unique

Each ballpark in Major League Baseball is unique. Every team wants its stadium to stand out. Some baseball stadiums have views of the ocean. Some parks feature statues of former players. Some parks even serve unusual food, such as burgers with pizza as the buns.

Some ballparks have long histories. The oldest ballpark still being used in the major league is Fenway Park. It is home to the Boston Red Sox. It opened in 1912. The left field wall stands 37 feet (11 m) high. It's called the Green Monster. Fans can buy tickets to sit above the Green Monster.

Wrigley Field is the second-oldest ballpark in operation. The home of the Chicago Cubs opened in 1914. One of the most unique features about Wrigley Field is the ivy that grows on the outfield wall.

The Miami Marlins' stadium features a retractable roof.

The Green Monster is the tallest outfield wall in the major leagues.

Some ballparks have special features that make attending games fun for fans. The Marlins play in Marlins Park. The stadium features two fish tanks behind home plate. The Tampa Bay Rays play at Tropicana Field, and they have live stingrays in the park. Fans can touch the rays in the 10,000-gallon (37,854-L) tank during games.

74
Number of years Wrigley Field was without lights after it opened in 1914.

- Fenway Park is the oldest stadium in the majors.
- Some stadiums have unique features such as fish tanks.
- Fans enjoy the unique experiences each stadium offers.

THINK ABOUT IT

Imagine you could design a new baseball stadium. What would the stadium look like? What features would you include? What do you think fans might enjoy?

Bright Young Stars Play in the Majors

Major League Baseball has lots of talented young players. Some of its brightest stars joined the big leagues at an early age.

Mike Trout was still a teenager when he first played in the majors. Trout is a center fielder who plays great defense. He can also hit for power. Bryce Harper also debuted as a 19-year-old. He's an athletic outfielder and an all-around hitter.

Bryce Harper was the National League MVP in 2015.

26.9

Average age of the Arizona Diamondbacks, the youngest team in the league, in 2016.

- Some players join the majors at an early age—even as teenagers.
- Mike Trout and Bryce Harper are among the best young stars.
- Young players such as Clayton Kershaw and Manny Machado have already seen great success.
- Kris Bryant helped lead the Cubs to a World Series.

was 20. He has already won two Gold Glove awards for fielding.

Kris Bryant joined the majors at age 23. Bryant was an All-Star in his first two seasons. He was also the National League Rookie of the Year in 2015. Bryant played an important role in the Cubs' 2016 World Series victory.

The future of baseball is bright with many talented young players. Who knows who the next exciting prospect will be?

Clayton Kershaw had just turned 20 years old when he first pitched in the big leagues. He went on to win three Cy Young Awards by the time he was 26. The Cy Young Award is given to the best pitcher in each league.

Manny Machado is another young star. He plays for the Baltimore Orioles. Machado debuted when he

Young star Manny Machado has already played in three All-Star games.

Baseball Records Are Legendary

Fans love baseball for its record-breaking performances. For instance, imagine someone not missing a single day of work for 16 years. That's what Cal Ripken Jr. did from 1982 to 1998. Ripken played 2,632 straight games. His streak is one of the most impressive records in baseball history.

Cy Young's win total as a pitcher is also amazing. Young won 511 games in his career. The award for the top pitcher in each league is named after him. Walter Johnson is second overall with 417 wins. Young's record likely won't be broken anytime soon. Bartolo Colon finished the 2016 season with 233 career wins. That was more than any active pitcher that year.

Joe DiMaggio holds another record that will probably last a long time. The New York Yankees star got a hit in 56 consecutive games in the 1941 season. As of 2016, no player has hit in more than 44 straight games since.

Cal Ripken Jr. never missed a single game in 16 years.

Pete Rose holds the record for most hits in MLB history. Ichiro Suzuki has more career hits than Rose. However, 1,278 of his hits came while playing in Japan. His hits do not break Rose's MLB record.

4,256
Number of Pete Rose's career hits.

- Baseball history is full of exciting record-breaking performances.
- Cal Ripken Jr. has the record for consecutive games played.
- Cy Young's and Joe DiMaggio's records may be hard to break.

Cy Young played for Boston in 1908.

THINK ABOUT IT

What would it be like to set a record in a sport or other activity? What skills might you need to set a record? What would it be like to have someone break your record?

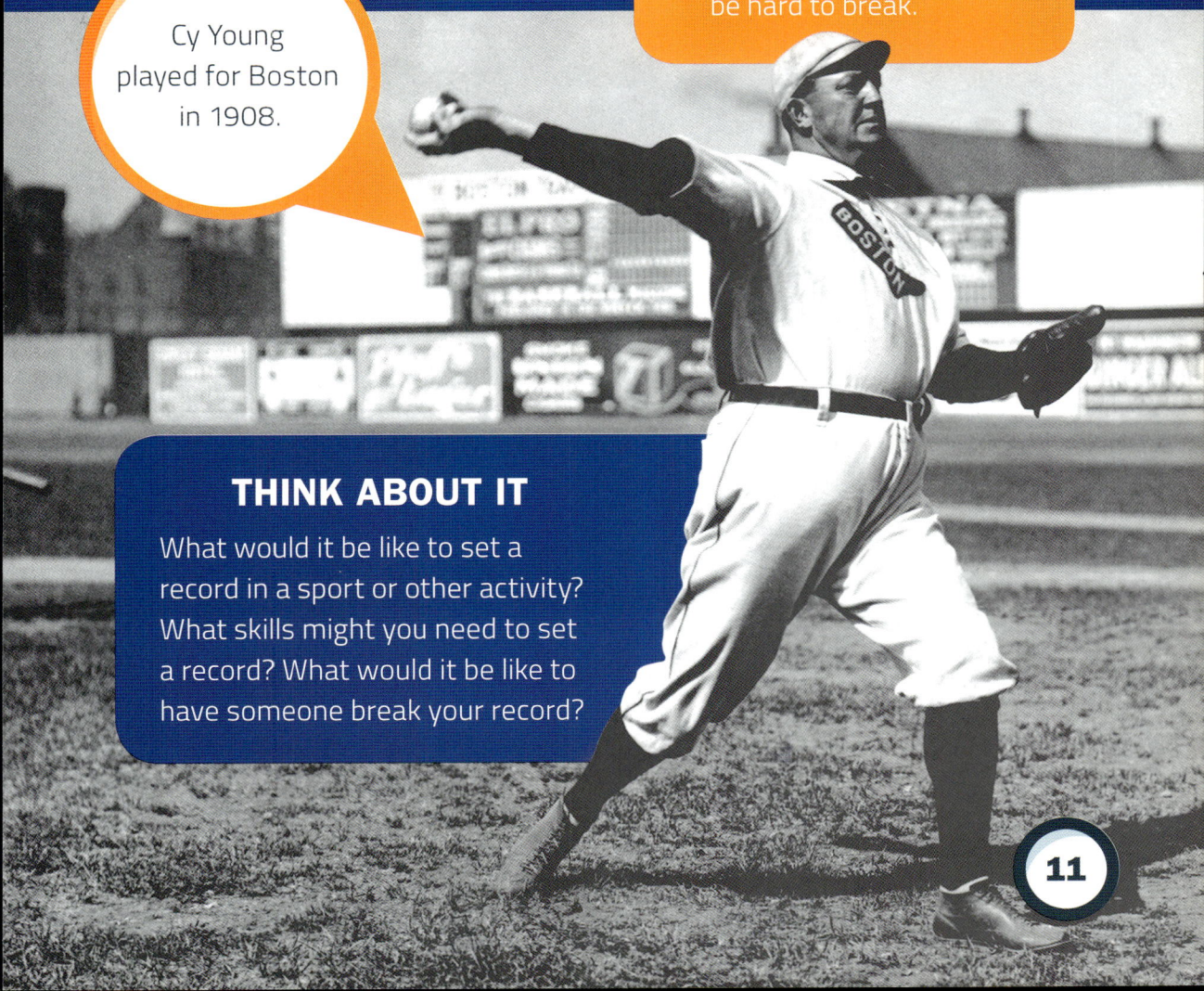

Spring Training Is a Warm Getaway

The MLB baseball season officially starts in April. Before then, teams practice and play preseason games in spring training. Spring training goes from the middle of February to the end of March. It's cold that time of year in many teams' hometowns. That's why all teams travel to warm locations instead.

Half of the teams train in Florida. The other half trains in Arizona. The group of teams that play in Florida are nicknamed the Grapefruit League. The Cactus League plays in Arizona. Some teams share the same spring training facilities and stadiums.

The spring training tradition dates back to 1870. That year, the Cincinnati Red Stockings trained in the warmer weather of New Orleans. The Washington Capitals were the first team to train in Florida. They prepared for the 1888 season in Jacksonville.

Warm temperatures help players get ready for the new season.

People wishing for a fun, warm vacation during spring break should check out a baseball schedule. Millions of fans come each year to watch spring training games.

Fans get excited for spring training. It means the official baseball season is getting closer. Also, spring training games are special experiences for fans. The stadiums are small and inviting. People can see their favorite players up close. They can watch players hitting in the batting cage or stand right next to pitchers as they warm up. Spring training is also a great spot to get autographs from favorite stars.

15,000

Seating capacity of Sloan Park in Mesa, Arizona, where the Cubs have spring training.

- Teams practice in spring training before the regular season starts.
- Spring training games are played in Florida and Arizona.
- Fans enjoy getting close to players at spring training games.

Fans get up close with players at spring training games.

Home Runs Are Exciting

Home runs are one of the most exciting plays in any sport. Some stadiums light off fireworks when the home team hits a home run. Others have fun celebrations for home runs.

The Milwaukee Brewers mascot slides down a slide. At Citi Field in New York, a giant apple rises in center field when the Mets hit homers. That's because New York is called the Big Apple.

Players who hit home runs often become fan favorites. Babe Ruth was a legendary home run hitter. He hit 714 home runs in his career. When he retired in 1935, Ruth had 400 more home runs than the second-place player. Hank Aaron eventually broke Ruth's record. Barry Bonds now has the all-time record with 762.

Home runs often make headlines. In 1998, Mark

Giancarlo Stanton slugs one out of the park.

- Babe Ruth was one of the first home run legends.
- Barry Bonds holds the career home run record at 762.
- Mark McGwire and Sammy Sosa competed in the home run chase of 1998.

HOME RUN DEBATES

Some home run records cause a lot of debate. Because home runs involve power, some sluggers have used illegal drugs to make themselves stronger. Bonds and McGwire admitted to using drugs that likely helped them hit home runs. Sosa was also suspected of taking illegal substances.

McGwire and Sammy Sosa both broke the record for most home runs in a season. The previous record was 61 by Roger Maris. McGwire finished with 70 homers. Sosa hit 66.

Today's top home run sluggers include Giancarlo Stanton of the Miami Marlins and Jose Bautista of the Toronto Blue Jays.

Babe Ruth was one of baseball's first home run heroes.

Yours Truly "Babe" Ruth

Cooperstown Celebrates Baseball History

The best players to ever play baseball are honored in one place. It's located in the tiny town of Cooperstown, New York.

The National Baseball Hall of Fame and Museum opened in 1939. That was three years after the first players were named to the hall of fame.

Fans often debate which players should be in the hall. However, that decision is up to certain baseball reporters and writers. Those writers vote for players to include in the hall of fame. Voting begins five seasons after a player has retired. For a player to be inducted, he must receive at least 75 percent of all votes cast. In 2016, Ken Griffey Jr.

312

Number of people who have been inducted into the Baseball Hall of Fame as of 2016.

- The hall of fame is in Cooperstown, New York.
- Baseball writers vote players into the hall of fame.
- Fans enjoy visiting the museum at Cooperstown.

FROM COOPERSTOWN TO HOLLYWOOD

Being a famous baseball star has its perks. Seventy-two hall of famers have appeared in movies. This includes Ken Griffey Jr., Mickey Mantle, and Reggie Jackson. Babe Ruth was in 11 movies, the most of any hall of fame player. Some players appeared as themselves. Other players acted as new characters.

received the highest percentage of votes at 99.32 percent.

Cooperstown is on many fans' must-see list. Approximately 300,000 people visit its museum each year. It includes a theater and famous photographs and items from games. The museum features a bronze plaque of each inductee's face. It's a special experience for baseball fans.

Baseball's best are honored in Cooperstown.

Baseball Is Popular around the Globe

Baseball is often called "America's national pastime." However, the sport is now popular around the world. People in many countries enjoy baseball. The major leagues have a team in Canada, the Toronto Blue Jays. Baseball is very popular in Japan, Venezuela, and the Dominican Republic.

A total of 864 players were in the major leagues to begin the 2016 season. Of those, 238 players were born outside the United States. That's more than 25 percent. The Dominican Republic had the most players of any international country with 82.

The World Baseball Classic (WBC) tournament shows how popular baseball is around the globe. The international tournament is played

Pedro Martinez (left) is one of many great players from the Dominican Republic.

BASEBALL IN JAPAN

Baseball has a long history in Japan. It was first played there in 1873. Baseball is now one of the most popular sports in Japan. Nippon Pro Baseball is the top league in Japan. Fans often chant and bang drums during games.

every four years. A total of 18 countries have played in the WBC since 2006. Japan won the first two tournaments. The Dominican Republic won the third in 2013.

Baseball will be an Olympic sport again in 2020. It was an Olympic sport from 1992 to 2008. But it was not in the Olympics in 2012 or 2016. South Korea beat Cuba

18

Number of countries outside the United States with players on an opening day roster in 2016.

- Baseball is popular around the world.
- In 2016, a quarter of MLB players were born outside the United States.
- Baseball will once again be an Olympic sport in 2020.

in 2008 to win the most recent Olympic baseball gold medal.

Team Japan won the first two WBC tournaments.

Baseball Is a Game of Numbers

Anyone who's bought baseball cards has probably looked at the players' statistics on the back. Statistics are the numbers used to measure how well a player performs. Statistics help fans know if a player is having a good season.

Some statistics measure how well a player hits. Home runs, runs batted in (RBI), and batting average are three examples. Batting average shows how often a player gets a hit. Pitcher statistics include wins, losses, and strikeouts.

Statistics are very important in baseball. They are used to decide which players receive certain

A scoreboard keeps fans up-to-date on statistics.

BASEBALL CARDS

Baseball cards are almost as old as baseball itself. The first cards were made in the 1880s. They did not have statistics on the back. They were just black-and-white pictures of players. Bubble gum was included with baseball cards in the 1930s. Some baseball cards are very valuable today. A 1909 card of hall of famer Honus Wagner sold for $2.8 million in 2007.

awards. The batting champion is the player with the highest batting average. A player who leads the league in home runs, RBI, and batting average is called the Triple Crown winner. It's difficult for a hitter to lead in all three areas. Miguel Cabrera was the most recent player to win it. He won it in 2012.

Miguel Cabrera's Triple Crown was the first since 1967.

17
Number of times in MLB history a hitter has won the Triple Crown.

- Statistics are numbers that help fans understand how well players are performing.
- Some common statistics include batting average and strikeouts.
- Many MLB awards are based on statistics.

Champions Win the World Series

The World Series is baseball's biggest event. It decides the major league champion each season.

Every fall, the best team from the American League and the best team from the National League play in the World Series. The series lasts anywhere from four to seven games. The first team to win four games is the champion.

The games are split between each team's stadium. Game 7, if needed, will be played at the stadium of the team with home-field advantage.

The World Series has been played since 1903. There have been many great moments in its history. Pittsburgh's Bill Mazeroski hit the first World Series–winning home

The Kansas City Royals celebrate winning the World Series.

WORLD SERIES

Players celebrate a Little League World Series victory.

run in 1960. His homer helped the Pirates beat the Yankees in Game 7. Joe Carter hit a home run in Game 7 to win the 1993 World Series for Toronto.

Yankees star Reggie Jackson earned the nickname "Mr. October" for his World Series success. He hit 10 home runs and had 24 RBI in five World Series. Jackson was also the World Series MVP in 1973 and 1977.

The MLB World Series is not the only popular World Series. Every year, Little League teams from all over the world try to get to the Little League World Series. It is played in Williamsport, Pennsylvania. College baseball players hope to play in the College World Series. That yearly event is held in Omaha, Nebraska.

1956

Year Yankee Don Larsen threw a perfect game in the World Series, not allowing a single batter on base.

- The World Series determines the MLB champion each season.
- The series has been played since 1903.
- Players such as Reggie Jackson have made World Series history.

Fans Love the All-Star Game

Think of the best baseball players in the big leagues. Now imagine those players facing off against each other in a game. That's what happens at the All-Star Game.

Fans vote to determine who will play in the All-Star Game. The American League players compete against the National League players. As of 2016, the American League and National League had played 80 times. The National League had won one more game than the American League.

The All-Star Game is often called the Midsummer Classic. It's played in the middle of the season, typically in July. The city that hosts the All-Star Game also has a FanFest. It's a great opportunity for fans to get autographs and meet legendary players.

The best of the best play in the MLB All-Star Game.

One day before the All-Star Game is the Home Run Derby. That's where the best sluggers try to hit as many homers as they can. The first Home Run Derby was held in 1985. In 2016, Giancarlo Stanton of the Miami Marlins beat Todd Frazier of the Cincinnati Reds.

FanFest is an exciting part of the All-Star Game.

61
Number of home runs Stanton hit in the 2016 Home Run Derby.

- Fans vote for players to be included in the All-Star Game.
- The American League players play against the National League players.
- The Home Run Derby is part of the festivities.

AN ALL-STAR TIE

The 2002 All-Star Game ended in a rare tie after 11 innings. Many people were disappointed. They believed the coaches and players didn't treat the All-Star Game like a real game. This inspired a rule change giving teams a reason to play for the win. Since 2003, the winning All-Star league has been awarded home-field advantage in the World Series.

Baseball Has Legendary Teams

Babe Ruth, Mickey Mantle, and Lou Gehrig are three of the most famous players in baseball history. They all played for the same team: the New York Yankees.

The Yankees are one of the most successful teams in MLB history. They have won more World Series titles than any other team. The Yankees have won 27 World Series. They have also played in the playoffs 52 times.

The Yankees' biggest and oldest rival is the Boston Red Sox. Boston became a team in 1901. Until 1908, they were called the Boston Americans. The Yankees and Red Sox have played more than 2,000 games against each other.

The Chicago Cubs are another legendary franchise. The Cubs have been a team since 1876. They were previously called the Colts, the Orphans, and the White Stockings.

Yankees from different decades celebrate their 27 championships.

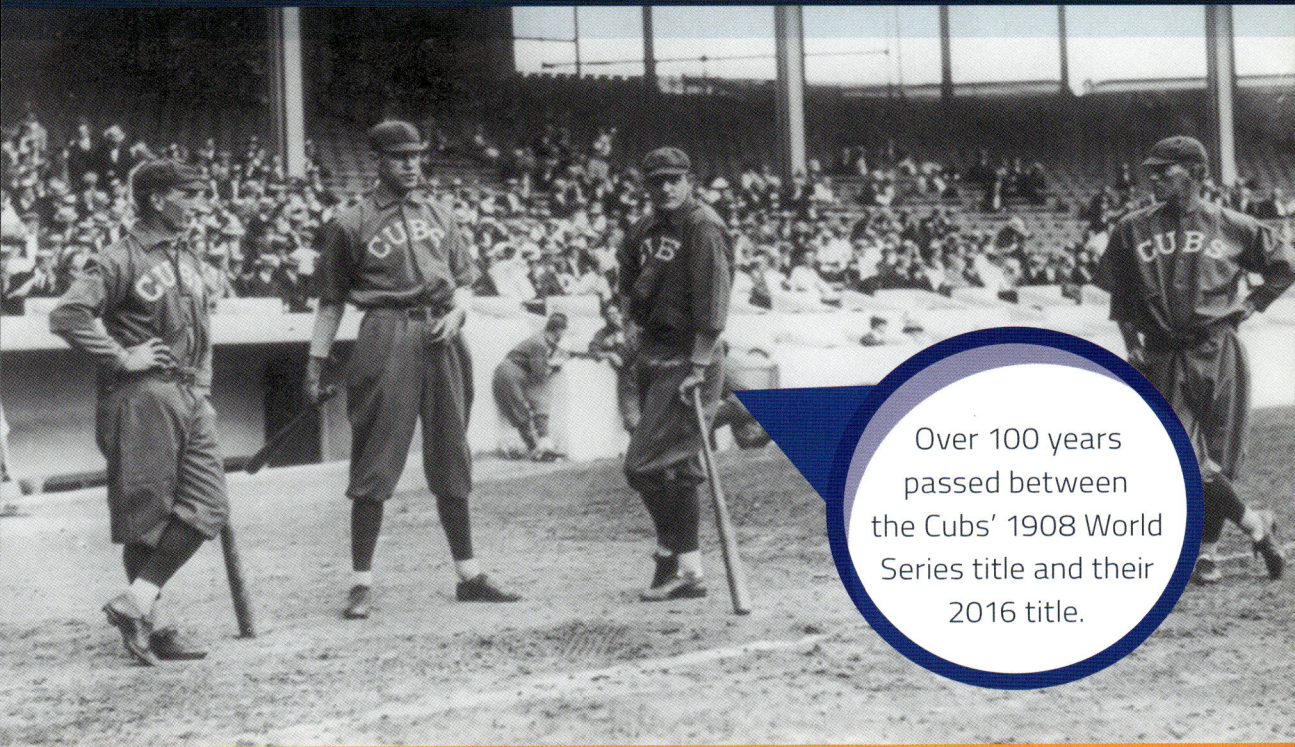

Over 100 years passed between the Cubs' 1908 World Series title and their 2016 title.

The Cubs won the World Series in 1908. But then it seemed they might never win it again. Some fans say that's because of the "Curse of the Billy Goat." According to tales, a fan with a pet goat was kicked out of a Cubs game during the 1945 World Series. In angry reply, he said the Cubs wouldn't win anymore. Fans were relieved when the Cubs finally won the championship in 2016.

THINK ABOUT IT

What makes a baseball team legendary? What would it be like to play for a legendary team? Would it be easier or harder than playing for a less famous team?

1,166
Number of times the Yankees have beaten the Red Sox.

- The New York Yankees have the most World Series titles.
- The Boston Red Sox are old rivals of the Yankees.
- The Chicago Cubs won the World Series in 1908 and 2016.

27

Fact Sheet

- The Yankees take pride in their 27 World Series championships. New York won its first World Series in 1923. Babe Ruth was the best player on that Yankees team. He hit 41 home runs that season. The Yankees won five straight World Series from 1949 to 1953.

- As of 2016, no one has played in more All-Star Games than Hank Aaron. He was a 21-time All-Star. Aaron's first All-Star Game was in 1954. His final year as an All-Star was 1976.

- Players who win the World Series get World Series rings. The rings are usually made of gold and gemstones. As of 2016, Yogi Berra won the most World Series rings of any player. He was on 10 World Series–winning teams.

In response to segregation rules in the early 1900s, black players formed their own baseball clubs known as the Negro Leagues. One organization, the Negro National League, was formed in 1920. The Negro Leagues broke apart once black players were allowed to play in the major leagues. This began with Jackie Robinson's debut in 1947. Many star Negro Leagues players such as Satchel Paige and Hank Aaron were also successful in the major leagues.

Glossary

debut
The first time a player appears in the major leagues.

executive
A person who works in the management of a team.

franchise
A sports team and the organization that runs it.

hall of fame
A select group of players considered the best to ever play the game.

home-field advantage
The right of a team to have an extra home game during a playoff series.

home run
A play in which a batter scores on his own hit, usually the result of the ball going over the outfield fence; when this happens, the batter and any runners on base score.

inductee
Someone inducted, or voted into, a hall of fame.

majors
Major League Baseball, the main professional baseball league in Canada and the United States.

perfect game
When a pitcher gets all 27 batters out in a game without anyone reaching base.

segregation
A form of discrimination that separates one group of people from another in society.

tradition
A pattern or set way of doing something over time.

For More Information

Books

Reavy, Kevin, and Ryan Spaeder. *Incredible Baseball Stats: The Coolest, Strangest Stats and Facts in Baseball History*. New York: Sports Publishing, 2016.

Syken, Bill. *Sports Illustrated Baseball's Greatest*. New York: Sports Illustrated, 2013.

Trexler, Phil. *Ballparks, Yesterday & Today*. Lincolnwood, IL: Publications International, 2011.

Visit 12StoryLibrary.com

Scan the code or use your school's login at **12StoryLibrary.com** for recent updates about this topic and a full digital version of this book. Enjoy free access to:

- Digital ebook
- Breaking news updates
- Live content feeds
- Videos, interactive maps, and graphics
- Additional web resources

Note to educators: Visit 12StoryLibrary.com/register to sign up for free premium website access. Enjoy live content plus a full digital version of every 12-Story Library book you own for every student at your school.

Index

About the Author

Tyler Mason studied journalism at the University of Wisconsin–Madison. He has covered professional and college sports in Minneapolis and Saint Paul, Minnesota, since 2009. He currently lives in Hudson, Wisconsin, with his wife.

READ MORE FROM 12-STORY LIBRARY

Every 12-Story Library book is available in many formats. For more information, visit 12StoryLibrary.com.